BUSINESS IS A
GAME

52 Rules to Make it Easier

MIKE MCKAY

SPECIAL FREE BONUS GIFT FOR YOU!

To help you achieve more success, there are FREE BONUS RESOURCES for you at: ActionCOACHWI.com

- This 3-part FREE video training series will show you how to attract more opportunities, achieve bigger goals & attract more abundance.

- In this FREE 3-part video training series, Business & Executive Coach Mike McKay reveals his Millionaire Entrepreneur Secrets for making massive money and working less in your business right NOW!

FREE $997 VALUE

- The first video reveals how people who Make More and Work Less Think and Act Differently Than Others, and gives you one powerful strategy for achieving more than ever before...STARTING NOW!

- The second video shows you how to market RIGHT – not harder, not smarter – RIGHT. Your messaging and your investments will bring you ideal clients right now!

- The third video shows you how to attract great employees for Your Team – even if employees are hard to find right now!

ActionCOACHWI.com/Free-Gift

Copyright © 2024

ALL RIGHT RESERVED. No part of this book or its associated ancillary materials may be reproduced or transmitted in any form or by any means, electronic or mechanical, including photocopying, recording, or by any informational storage or retrieval system without permission from the publisher.

DISCLAIMER AND/OR LEGAL NOTICES

While all attempts have been made to verify information provided in this book and its ancillary materials, neither the author nor publisher assumes any responsibility for errors, inaccuracies or omissions and is not responsible for any financial loss by customers in any manners. Any slights of people or organizations are unintentional. If advice concerning legal, financial, accounting or related matters in needed, the services of a qualified professional should be sought. This book and its associated ancillary materials, including verbal and written training, in not intended for use as a source of legal, financial or accounting advice. You should be aware of the various laws governing business transactions or other business practices in your particular geographic location.

The author has made every effort to ensure the accuracy of the information within this book was correct at time of publication. The author does not assume and hereby disclaims any liability to any party for any loss, damage, or disruption caused by errors or omissions, whether such errors or omissions result from accident, negligence, or any other cause.

Any examples, stories, references or case studies are for illustrative purposes only and should not be interpreted as testimonies and/or examples of what reader and/or consumers can expect. Any statements, strategies, concepts, techniques, exercises and ideas in this information, materials and/or seminar training offered are simply opinion or experience, and thus should not be misinterpreted as promises.

This book is dedicated to the entrepreneur community; the amazing people that make up small, medium and large business who make a massive impact in the communities they operate in, and to the families and communities that support them. I'd also like to thank my family, friends and colleagues, whose belief in our cause energizes us to do our work everyday. And finally, to our clients—you guys rock. Thank you for changing the world.

THE IDEAL PROFESSIONAL SPEAKER FOR YOUR NEXT EVENT!

Any organization that wants to develop their people to become "extraordinary," needs to hire Mike for a keynote and/or workshop training!

To Contact Or Book Mike To Speak:
actioncoachwi.com./speakers

CONTENTS

A Message For You 13
INTRODUCTION 15

TIPS

1 — The single most powerful thing to do for your business 20
2 — Stubbornness 21
3 — Systems and Repetition 22
4 — Limiting Beliefs 23
5 — Hindsight Bias 24
6 — Why don't they buy this, it's the cheapest? 25
7 — "The enemy of great is good" 27
8 — Decisiveness 28
9 — Speed is Life 29
10 — Should you go 100 MPH all the time? 30
11 — I Know 31
12 — Money 32
13 — Identity 33
14 — Engagement is a Two-Way Street 35
15 — Professional Selling 36
16 — Can't get other people to do your pushups 38
17 — Be x Do = Have 39
18 — Be x Do = Have — Part 2 40
19 — Specific Results 41
20 — The only Failure… 42
21 — Money has no morals 43
22 — Who Owns Your Culture? 45

23 — How Many Things Can You Do?..........46
24 — Gratitude..........47
25 — How Much Work Do You Do on You?..........48
26 — Magic Isn't Easy..........49
27 — We Can't..........50
28 — Transparency..........51
29 — Action Addiction..........52
30 — A 16 Beats a 1..........53
31 — Hiring..........54
32 — I'm struggling to sell..........55
33 — And now this random comment... Hate..........57
34 — Are You Planning on Working Tomorrow?..........58
35 — What, Exactly Are Your Competitors Doing?..........60
36 — Learn from Napoleon..........62
37 — How to stop a lion..........63
38 — Persuasion..........64
39 — The Kool Aid..........65
40 — I Choose to Indulge in..........66
41 — Sprinting versus Endurance..........68
42 — Experience..........69
43 — Evidence Based Decision Making..........71
44 — Your Business Called. It Wants Help..........72
45 — Lessons from The Golf Course..........73
46 — Go Small and Go Fast..........74
47 — Breakthrough..........76
48 — Perturbation..........78
49 — There is Always Pain..........79

50 — Why?..81
51 — The Quality of Your Output..82
52 — Clean Your Mind 83
53 — Additional resources 85

A MESSAGE FOR YOU

BUSINESS HAS RULES, a scorecard, and teams, the very definition of a game. Here are 52 basic rules to help you play this amazing game at a higher level on a continuous basis.

Following these will allow you to make more money, by working less, every time you learn and execute one.

Good luck on your journey, and contact us when you want someone by your side to make it as easy as possible.

INTRODUCTION

I LEFT THE Army in 1991. At the time, all I wanted to do was work for the biggest company I could find so I went to work for a division of Philip Morris called Post Cereals. Yes, I became one of the many people who made Grape-Nuts.

But what I learned there, started a journey of learning leadership and business that has lasted 30+ years, and becomes more fun every year.

It didn't start out that way. I felt the pressure and stress of "time" when I worked at Post. When I went to NewellRubbermaid, I felt the pressure and stress of KPIs, and added non-stop travel for the company for 16 years. I thought I loved it. That it was what I wanted to do.

But I was having a really tough time "fitting in" with my peers. I thought they were making things a lot harder on us as an executive team than necessary, and they all thought I was lazy. This came to a head in 2012, when I got myself fired.

It was a mess. So much so, that during interviews with future companies, all that was running through my head was "I can't work this way anymore." I was at a turning point for my life.

My turning point was threefold:

1. I learned there was a whole industry focused on becoming a better leader and business owner, and that it's a sign of strength and maturity, to seek help
2. I invested in myself — hired a coach to guide me through my blind spots and the areas where I wasn't strong
3. I LEARNED THE RULES. It wasn't that I was playing the wrong game. I was following the wrong rules. Making things harder than they needed to be.

Learning the rules changed everything for me, and it can for you, too.

If any of this resonates with you — you're playing as hard as you can, but wondering if it is ever going to get easier, or you're always feeling torn between your family and your business — then you're going to love this book, because you'll learn the rules of the game.

How to grow your business in a way that's both sustainable and gives you back your time and energy for your family, your health, and YOU.

Today I own a thriving, profitable, globally award-winning business that gives leaders the kind of help and support I wish I'd had all those years ago. And I do it all in 40 hours a week, with lots of vacation time in cool places around the world, and plenty of money and time to enjoy the things and people I love.

That's what it's all about. Let's get started.

RULES OF THE GAME OF BUSINESS

1
THE SINGLE MOST POWERFUL THING TO DO FOR YOUR BUSINESS

Choose a niche and own it.

Scary, maybe difficult, hard work to define it, blah, blah, blah.

There are hundreds of reasons that people fear choosing a niche.

What does Coca Cola do? Nike? Apple?

Before you start tossing line extensions out at me, evaluate them over time. Yes, Nike did golf equipment. It failed. How about the Apple Newton? Ever seen Coke sell something besides beverages?

How about General Motors? Have you bought an Oldsmobile lately? Ever have a GM washer/dryer?

Niche. We all need ONE to dominate and we all need to walk away from bright shiny pennies.

2
STUBBORNNESS

Why, oh why, would someone continue to follow a path that does not go where they want to go?

The throw away answer is that it's easier to keep doing what you've always done. I think there's a saying about that...

The less easy answer is they are too stubborn to think there may be a different way.

Young kids are awesome at finding another way. Any other way. To get what they want. They're not stuck in beating their heads against the same wall time and time again.

Why are adults?

Well, I think it's because we don't want to do the hard work of figuring out where it is we want to go.

One of our clients admitted being afraid of what might happen when all her work pays off and her business is two or three times as large as it is right now.

But she said she's going to do it anyhow. Her last piece of stubbornness just melted away.

Has yours?

3
SYSTEMS AND REPETITION

We have clients who are required to do a cash flow forecast for us as part of their coaching program.

This single tool is the most critical aspect of financial control over a business. Yes we need the P&L, Balance Sheet, and Statement of Cash Flows, but the cash flow forecast is literally a lifesaver.

I know this because one of our clients stopped doing this on a weekly basis. Because they were flush with cash. And they had repeated the task so many times that they got bored.

You can guess that they ran out of money.

And you can probably guess that the fix, just as fast, was to get back to doing the weekly cash flow forecast and turning it in.

Look, running a great business can be a boring endeavor. Do the things that work repetitively and don't stop.

And just when you think that it's too boring to do it again, so you stop, it's going to bite you right in the ass!

Don't do that to yourself—keep doing the systemic things that make you successful. So that you can spend the time previously spent fighting fires working on your business to make it even greater!

4
LIMITING BELIEFS

"That's the way it is."

"We could never do that here."

"I can't make a million dollars"

Look, I'm not in the business of telling you how much money you need to make, or how many vacations you need. I happen to believe the best person to make those decisions is you.

But I AM in the business of wrecking limiting beliefs.

There is no law against making a lot of money. Or taking a lot of vacation.

There is lots of head trash around making a lot of money.

"Well, the rich people live over there. They're not like us."

What a load of shit. "They" are exactly like us. They simply don't believe the limiting rules you might be telling yourself every day.

5
HINDSIGHT BIAS

There is some thought that experience retroactively rewires your brain.

A group of people were interviewed before the last election. They were recorded. The ones who picked Clinton to win were interviewed again a few weeks later.

Every one of them, even when they were played back the recording of their interview saying they picked Clinton, said "yeah, but I knew Trump was going to win". Really?

It sounds like "I KNEW I should have", or "See, that's exactly what I thought was going to happen".

What if we really can never go back to the time before a decision? What if our brain really is protecting us from egocide and admitting we were wrong on the big things?

Seems like the only way forward is to decide and execute. Especially if, in hindsight, our brain is going to tell us we knew it all along…

A fascinating, but dry, book on this subject and many others is *Thinking Fast and Slow* by Daniel Kahneman.

6
WHY DON'T THEY BUY THIS, IT'S THE CHEAPEST?

"More on emotion? Come on, Mike, just tell me what to do."

I actually heard this quote from one of my peeps.

He's a salesperson and he keeps going back to assigning the numeric logic to the decision and keeps failing to persuade.

Me–"What kind of car do you drive?"

Him — "Mercedes."

Me — "Why?"

Him — "Because it makes me feel like I'm successful enough to drive a Mercedes."

Me — "Well, you know there is no logic to that decision. You should have bought a Chevy; they are a lot cheaper."

Him — "Mike, there's more to buying a car than price."

Me — "Huh."

Him — "Huh, what? What are you getting at?"

I'm sure you've all just picked up the lesson, but I'll clarify if not.

People do NOT buy on price — ever — in at least one area of their lives. Cars, watches, clothes, organic food, houses, bikes, etc., etc., etc.

The question is, what are you trying to sell them, and is it an area of their life that specific person values?

If it's not, best find out soon and go sell to someone who cares.

7
"THE ENEMY OF GREAT IS GOOD"

I heard this quote the other day and I wondered exactly what that means. Yesterday I said that everyone buys on value, not price, in at least one area of their lives.

And in that area that you value, this applies.

I don't want good golf clubs; I want great golf clubs. I don't want a good car; I want a great car.

Does that necessarily make a good car bad? Not to me — I'm just not going to buy it unless I perceive it as great.

I also believe that the companies who do things "good" will never be great companies. If good is the objective, we get Chevy's. If great is the objective, we get Teslas.

Which do you prefer? Your customers want great. Do you truly understand what that means to them?

8
DECISIVENESS

I made an offer a few weeks ago to a client.

The salient point is I offered them a "fast action scholarship" of around 8% if they committed within 3 days.

They didn't.

When they did decide, they wanted the fast action scholarship anyhow. They used the old "well if you were willing to sell at that price then, you'll be willing to sell at that price now" negotiating tactic.

The price never changed. They chose to pass on the fast action incentive. So the price is still the price.

He didn't get it.

Look, there is a concrete and specific cost of indecision. Usually you can ignore that cost because no one sticks it in your face. I just made it a little more obvious in this case.

Where are you paying the price for indecision?

9
SPEED IS LIFE

Here's a phrase from the way back department.

Look, if something is a good idea, it's a good idea to do it right now.

Don't skip the part where you choose priorities, but if something is a good idea and a high priority, then right now is the time to do it. Not next week. Not a month from now.

Right. F*!#ing. Now

10
SHOULD YOU GO 100 MPH ALL THE TIME?

I listened to a guy who purports to do the "same thing" we do.

He also proposes that every entrepreneur should be working on at least 3 businesses at the same time.

Which is exactly what we DON'T do.

Look, focus is more powerful than random. Action is more powerful than inaction.

Focused action is the most powerful place to operate from. That does not mean run around like your hair is on fire. It means do the right thing, and enough of it to hit your goals, and then do no more.

We do not advocate doing nothing. We also don't advocate trying to do everything.

As an old friend of mine says, "focus, pickle!"

11
I KNOW

One of our core mindset principles is that the two simple words "I Know" stop adult learning.

It doesn't sound like that in adults though. It sounds more like "that won't work here" or "we tried that before and it didn't work" or "you don't understand my industry".

All BS.

When I hear those phrases, what I really hear is "we had these amazing learning opportunities and instead of taking advantage of them, we just ignored all the learning so we could stay right where we are comfortable."

That's an active choice NOT to learn from experiences. Seems foolish.

12
MONEY

Lots of discussions with people about money recently.

An interesting phenomenon is popping up regularly, and that is negative beliefs about money.

One person even shared with me that they would like to become filthy rich.

Do you think that is going to work out for that person? I mean, their subconscious can hear words like that, and often focuses on the filthy part at the expense of the rich part. Because if their belief about wealth is that it's filthy, their subconscious is never going to let them get there.

See what I mean?

What are your beliefs about money? Write down the first few things that come to mind, to make sure that they are positive. If not, it's a simple choice to replace them with positive thoughts.

Here's one to try on — the universe pays me directly for the value I provide. If I want more money, I simply need to add more value to people.

13
IDENTITY

I used to think I was just who I was.

Then I learned about the identity iceberg and that even something that I thought was unchangeable, is absolutely changeable.

When I had a job, I always thought of myself as the smartest guy in the room. It was kind of expected in that environment that to be the top dog meant holding everyone else back to some degree.

I didn't even realize I was doing it until my coach asked me this question.

Was it my objective to be an absentee husband, a shitty father, and a questionable leader?

Wow. Have that thrown at you and see how it feels.

But I had to admit that he was right. I spent 170 nights a year, on average, away from my family and when I was home all I could think about was going back to work. It consumed me. Seemingly 24 hours a day. And it was not what I wanted to be.

So I had to dig deep. I had to do the work of questioning who I wanted to be, what kind of husband and father I wanted to be, and what kind of leader I wanted to be. I'm not sure how it happened but I ended up deciding that my best option was to collect people for my team that were smarter than me and earn the right to lead them.

So now, my identity is, that I'm the best talent collector on the planet. My life is easier in many, many ways because now I see tons of opportunity to help people get better at what they do. And the side effect is my role becomes easier, and a hell of a lot more fun!

What's your identity?

14
ENGAGEMENT IS A TWO-WAY STREET

We occasionally get to work with a company on employee engagement.

It's a blast. Did you know that 72% of all workers in the US are either unengaged or actively disengaged from their jobs?

That means the ¾ths of the work force is just killing time when they are on your payroll.

But it doesn't have to be that way. You can create an environment where they will engage for you. And engaged employees are between 42-70% more productive that unengaged employees.

So yes, that means that the potential to avoid having to hire more people, which is a challenge in today's economy, may rest in just engaging the employees you have to let them be more productive.

And usually, all you have to do is ask!

15
PROFESSIONAL SELLING

During an interesting discussion with a client today, she asked "how do I get my salespeople to be more effective at selling?"

Great question.

I was terrified of selling when I first realized I would need to sell myself and my business.

Talk about a BFO — I'm not sure how I missed that connection, but I didn't make it when I bought my business.

I had no choice but to become a salesperson.

Here's the upside — selling is a problem-solving process. That's all it is. And I happen to be good at problem solving.

So, what I decided was to work with my coach to design and evaluate every step of how I run a sales meeting. I tested each one, with his help, refined them, practiced again and again, and now I can sell at a very high rate of 77% closing.

That was all work I was willing to do, and skills I was willing to work on because I made the decision to become a professional salesperson.

So the question back to her was "what makes you think they want to be more effective at selling?" Because if they don't want to become great, they won't.

If they do want to become more effective, then step one is to give them a process to follow, test, measure and improve.

What is your sales process?

16
CAN'T GET OTHER PEOPLE TO DO YOUR PUSHUPS

"You can't hire someone else to do your pushups for you" — Jim Rohn

Wow. On those days when you wish things were easier and wish that you didn't have to do whatever it is in front of you that you need to do, remember Jim Rohn's quote. You won't get any benefit from someone else doing the hard work that you need to do.

17
BE X DO = HAVE

I'm going to hit on Be x Do = Have over the next few days.

First, let's talk about what your "be" means.

The person you are is made up of your skills, beliefs, values, and your core identity. And those are not things that we can see.

But I can say this — to get a different result than you are getting right now, will require that you "be"come something that you aren't right now.

That may mean developing new skills. It may mean divorcing yourself from some beliefs that aren't serving you — like in my case, that I wasn't a salesperson. Becoming something different may even take the extremely hard work of evaluating and changing your values.

Scary.

But the formula holds true. The person that you are, times the things that you do, equals the results you have in all aspects of your life — health, relationships, finances, etc.

If you want a different result, where will you start first?

18
BE X DO = HAVE – PART 2

Let's talk "have" today.

How do you feel when you open your wallet, or look at your bank account? How about when you evaluate your relationships?

Great? Not so great?

If those are results, meaning that they really are the outcome of who you are times what you are doing (here's a hint — they absolutely are that result) then what are you willing to change to get a different result in your bank account or wallet or relationship, etc.?

Notice I didn't ask what can you change. I asked what are you willing to change.

We can change anything we want. There is so much information in the world on how to get better at anything — health, relationships, finances, etc. — that this is not a question of "can".

It's a question of "willing".

What are you willing to do to get the results you would like to pursue?

19
SPECIFIC RESULTS

We know "more" money is not an actual goal.

How specific are you with what you want to create? The less specific you are, the less result you're going to get.

I don't even know how it happens, but the vaguer your results expectations are, the measlier the results you'll actually get.

Pick the number. Set your RAS. Do the work.

And then don't let any of those bullshit ideas about money from yesterday into your head or all that work will be for naught.

20
THE ONLY FAILURE...

One of our core mind set beliefs is that the only failure is the failure to participate.

What exactly does that mean?

Well, you know how to walk right? So when you were a very young child you learned the benefits of Try, Try Again. Because that is how you learned to walk.

But what has happened since then?

In school, you were taught to raise your hand when you "knew" the answer, not when you were trying to figure out the answer.

What is that message?

It seems like that message is don't try to do something unless you already know how to do it. That makes no sense. How can you possibly learn to do anything if you won't try it until you know how to do it?

And the message behind the only failure is the failure to participate, is the same message. You only fail when you choose not to learn any more. When you decide your comfort zone is so comfortable that you stop taking risks. When you won't try to answer a question unless you already know the answer.

And that means that the only failure is the failure to learn.

21
MONEY HAS NO MORALS

I read an article by a guy named Dexter Abraham. I read Dexter's stuff because he's the only guy I read who regularly swears as much as me. AND — he tells the unvarnished truth about the ups and downs of a durable business.

Also, he doesn't publish often, so when he does it's worth reading.

He summarizes writings and events by Dan Kennedy in this particular article.

My mind was blown in a few ways, but there are two ideas that are staying with me.

First is that money goes where it's happiest.

Wow. We all know someone who makes a quick buck in some scummy fashion and that money is gone almost as fast as it showed up. It's not happy hanging out with scum. I hadn't ever thought of it that way in the past.

And it's perfectly happy hanging with the Kardashians.

BTW, you all know we've done work with Michael Losier on Law of Attraction. Dexter's summary fits perfectly in with that info as well. Scary good, actually. Because the other idea, was a killer summary of something I have learned before which is the idea of poverty consciousness. Not awareness, but consciousness. And again, with Law of Attraction — I attract into my life more of anything I give my energy, focus and attention to — whether positive or negative.

Poverty consciousness is negative focus. So, you'll attract more poverty. Shit.

22
WHO OWNS YOUR CULTURE?

I've worked for a couple of big companies back when I could hold a job.

At one of them, my staff was complaining about the culture in the business and specifically in two of the departments that we were responsible for.

"Who creates the culture?" I asked.

Blank stares. I think they got the point.

And then we decided to change the culture, which meant we had to change our behavior. Ultimately it meant I had to change MY behavior because I was the most senior leader.

While it was tough to do, it worked as planned.

And so I ask you — if you own a company, are a member of a senior team of a company, are an executive, a team member, or any other role in a company, your family, your social circle, etc., aren't you too responsible for that culture?

And if you are, shouldn't you work on it instead of accepting the bad parts of it?

Because only you can effect change.

23
HOW MANY THINGS CAN YOU DO?

I am really good at what we call coaching from the stage.

I can make sure everyone in a room gets a pertinent message that they need to hear, really no matter the topic.

Because I have trained with the best in the business at that skill — Brad Sugars.

The next best skill I have is much, much lower on the skill rating.

If I coach 100 people at a time, seems like that is more valuable than coaching one at a time.

When I work on secondary skills, it has a microscopic effect on results. So why the hell does everyone say work on your weaknesses?

We say work in your strengths! Because you likely only have one or two where all your superpower resides.

Why divert effort?

24
GRATITUDE

I admit, I haven't always lived in gratitude.

Why did that guy get the promotion instead of me?

Why does this seem so easy for her (remember yesterday's note — it's because I was working in a weakness, not a strength)?

Man, I wish I had...

Turns out all those focused my RAS on lack. And when you focus your RAS, you get more of whatever you focus on.

Now I try, of course I'm not perfect, to get up and say Thank You for everything, all day.

When someone cuts me off, I TRY to think thank you for making me practice patience. That one doesn't always, or even often if I'm truthful, work. But I'm testing how I feel when it does work.

And when I think grateful thoughts, more of what I'm grateful for shows up.

Might be worth a try.

25
HOW MUCH WORK DO YOU DO ON YOU?

What gets me every time is one simple question. Are you ready to up your game?

Because if so, you need to actually up your game.

Get better–at fewer things, probably.

Delegate more, test more, execute more, take more action in fewer areas.

So the work on how to do that is the work. We all have the same amount of time. We all have the same opportunity to be better. We all have the same excuses for where we are in our journeys.

And they're all ok.

But I want to up my game.

So it's back to the hard work of working on me!

Thank you for reading along on my journey — I hope you're working on you, too!

26
MAGIC ISN'T EASY

I'm reading the manuscript of a book.

The initial story is called The Miser's Dream. You can see it on YouTube, but the short version is making money appear out of thin air.

For the magician, this looks easy. Because you don't have to watch the thousands of hours of practice that it takes to learn how to effectively palm multiple coins to do the illusion.

Same thing for business. For the "overnight" success stories, you just didn't have to see all the failures and practice that went in to learning how to make something look easy.

But as a business owner — you have to do all that work to make your business look easy. Learn all the stuff, make lots of the mistakes, and do all the things.

We recommend taking the shortest path through all that learning. But the path isn't one day long.

Keep that in mind when your business is frustrating you and you look longingly at a peer making it look easy. And remember, you just didn't have to watch their thousands of hours of practice, like you have to experience your own.

27
WE CAN'T

Whose responsibility is it when employees of a business say, "we can't" instead of asking "how can we?"

Well, if you're the owner look in the mirror.

Being a leader is a non-stop role. There is never a day off when you can just say "F*ck It, I am going to be a victim today."

Because your people are always watching you. And it's quite possible that one or more of your employees only sees you on the day that you are whining and complaining. So in their minds, that's who you are.

They don't see the other 9 days where you are positive and inspirational — only the day you threw in the towel.

Which to them means, it's ok for them to act that way also. Hey, you're the leader, you set the pace.

But here's the reward anyhow — when you take responsibility for everything that happens, it's a lot more fun to move forward.

Yes, you'll have setbacks. Yes, something is going to go wrong. Of course, someone is going to quit at the wrong time.

Those are all opportunities to lead! So take them.

28
TRANSPARENCY

I just read a really cool thought.

A truly great leader becomes transparent. Not to show their team that they are an open book.

Rather, so the team sees through them to the core of the whole company! So that their team sees everything that the company is trying to achieve, why it matters, and their role, through their leader's transparency!

Wow.

Mind -> Blown!

Are you transparent, in that manner?

29
ACTION ADDICTION

This is a term I picked up in Darren Hardy's Insane Productivity Course.

And when he said it, I could feel it in my bones.

The Thing that I need to wean myself off of.

We're coming off a really busy week. We had a temporary admin for a while, and she needed lots of help with the stuff that had to be done for quarterly planning that we were hosting. I knew that.

But instead of clearing my schedule, so I could work on what was important, I ADDED more meetings, calls, and activities to do. Even while I knew that the right thing to do would be to clear my schedule and help her get us ready for Friday.

Huh. Stupid choice.

I heard another coach say the most elegant form of being lazy is to be busy. And in retrospect, I have to admit it was lazy of me to take those meetings and not focus on the one thing. It certainly made me feel good to be busy. But on Friday, it also made me feel like the whole week leading up to it was self-inflicted stupidity.

Don't do that to yourself.

30
A 16 BEATS A 1

How is it possible that a team ranked 16th in its bracket beat a team ranked 1st?

I'm not a basketball coach, but what I saw Virginia display seemed like a ton of cognitive dissonance. Not believing that what was happening to them could be happening to them. They just kept looking at that bad thing, and just kept getting more of it.

So they never got back in the game.

I see that happen to business owners occasionally also. Something goes off the rails, they don't believe it, and then stare at it, causing more of the same shit to happen.

Law of attraction works — you attract more of whatever you give your focus, energy, and attention too, whether negative or positive.

"Never look at the wall, look at the track, your car goes where your eyes go" Mario Andretti.

Are your eyes on the prize? Or are they on the few small hurdles in the way, making them bigger and harder to get over?

31
HIRING

We just presented our hiring process to a bunch of tradespeople a couple of weeks ago.

The most common response? Yeah, but that won't work in our industry.

Here's a newsflash — we work with customers in all those industries. In fact, nearly a hundred industries over the past 6 years,

And the hiring process works in every single one of them.

So, if your thoughts are that hiring is nearly impossible in our industry, or that I can't find good people, or my favorite, "Mike, you don't understand...", maybe it's time to look in the mirror and repeat these 7 magic words.

We all get exactly who we deserve.

If you can't find people, we just need you to become a better employer. Or a better boss.

And when you get this right, the right people in the right quantity will always be there to work for you.

Or at least in the hundred industries we've worked with, that has always been the case…

32
I'M STRUGGLING TO SELL...

Tuesday a person I was talking to actually said those words.

"Well," I said, "it's because you keep setting yourself up for that to happen."

"Mike, I would never do that!"

"Really? I just listened to a sales call you recorded, and you said, 'you probably don't have enough money to do this, but if you did...'. So you told them not to buy from you."

"Well, I figured this was expensive and most reasonable people wouldn't buy it."

Well, you figured right, Sparky. And not only did you figure right, you made it happen by telling them not to buy!

I've said before that we don't market to ourselves.

We also don't buy from ourselves.

If you are assigning value decisions to the people you are talking to, you're never going to be great at sales.

Here's the tip — let them tell you the value of the product or service by simply saying yes or no. Don't predispose them to a no because you wouldn't spend that kind of money.

Or get out of the field and go sell something you believe in.

33
AND NOW THIS RANDOM COMMENT... HATE

"I hate those guys. I hate that team. I think that person is an asshole. I can't believe what a moron such and such is. She needs to be fired! I can't believe that person still works here."

What's the point in all that? How exactly does that make YOUR life better. And how, exactly, does that add energy, joy, passion and riches to you and your life.

I'm not going to go such a short distance as to say love everyone else. I mean there is organized religion for that and all.

I am just going to remind us all that the energy put into hate could be going to something that is positive and useful for you and your loved ones. It could be used to do something good for the world. It could be used to create the most amazing life you can possibly imagine.

'Cuz the hate isn't getting you anywhere anyhow.

Oh, yeah. Remember one other thing—our friend Law of Attraction? You get more of whatever you give your energy, focus, and attention to whether negative or positive.

Fastest way to get more hatred into your life turns out to be focusing on hating.

34
ARE YOU PLANNING ON WORKING TOMORROW?

I was crushed on St Patrick's Day, 2011 when my dad called me.

He said my mom had been killed in a car crash.

Fuck. Of course, I didn't believe it. I have this crystal-clear memory of feeling like I had been punched in the gut, bending over my desk wanting to puke in my office. My world changed that day. My whole family's world changed–especially my dad.

I don't want sympathy. Worse has happened to many, many people.

My mom reinvented herself a dozen times while I was growing up. First a stay at home mom. Then a caterer. Then owning a restaurant. Then finishing college when she was 60 and starting a piano studio. Then finally taking the art classes she had always wanted to take.

She didn't really look back, and always said move on to the next version of you, so you can live a great life.

I think I ignored that comment 100 times.

I challenge you to think about what you are doing tomorrow, and whether you are moving toward an amazing life full of energy, joy, passion and riches. Or just living the same day, over and over again, because it's easier not to change.

Just because you're planning to go to work like usual tomorrow doesn't mean that's going to happen.

35
WHAT, EXACTLY ARE YOUR COMPETITORS DOING?

The construction industry in Southern Wisconsin is on fire. Volume and pace that is unbelievable. Labor shortages. Companies that went out of business in the recession can't even come back in to being because there are no people.

And now, well, Foxconn.

Cool, eh?

What's not cool are the companies who are not participating in the current building boom. I don't mean not getting the work–they are getting work.

I mean not getting the pricing they should be getting.

There are companies who are doubling their charged labor rate, and still closing deals. There are companies putting 5, 10 or even 20% price overrides on top of their bids and still closing deals.

And then there are a surprisingly large number of companies who aren't doing anything like that. They are signing deals that will take until the end of the year to complete, stressing out because their customers aren't happy that it will take that long.

And the owners "feel" bad.

Well, Sparky. There is a reason for the saying "make hay when the sun shines". Your competitors are earning higher pricing, which is making them financially stronger and thus able to withstand what happens in the future.

Are you keeping up with them? Or are you going to be run over by them?

36
LEARN FROM NAPOLEON

"There are no bad soldiers under a good general"
—*Napoleon Bonaparte*

Just another way of saying Life is a Mirror. Bad team? Bad leader.

Yep–period.

37
HOW TO STOP A LION

Ever notice that lion tamers can walk into a cage with a lion and not get eaten.

How is that possible?

Well, notice also that they carry a stool with four legs on it. They hold those four legs toward the lion. The lion sees that as four distinct threats, doesn't know which one poses the biggest problem, so they shut down completely and don't attack the tamer.

Recently, you've probably also read about or seen that people jump into lion cages and get eaten. They don't have multiple threats with them. They are a single threat. The lion knows what to do with one threat. It attacks.

How do you assess the world right now? Are you focused on the most important thing, and attacking it, or do you see so many opportunities that you are shutting down?

38
PERSUASION

Can you persuade someone to your point of view?

Maybe it's easier to ask whether you ever have persuaded someone to change their point of view to match yours?

On the other hand, have you ever invited someone to participate in a conversation where you share ideals and ideas?

It's a lot easier to do that.

Marketing is similar, whether you like it or not. If someone doesn't believe in you or what you're selling, it will be virtually impossible to "sell" them.

The easier path is to find the people that believe what you believe and are willing to go where you are going. Those folks will buy from you again and again.

And you find them through marketing.

39
THE KOOL AID

Do you believe that things are so easy you can do some hack that makes you an overnight success, or your business an overnight success?

There aren't any.

There is, however, an easier way.

Pick a path, or as Jim Rohn said, a philosophy, and implement that philosophy in its entirety.

Every step, no skipping around and just doing the parts you want. You have to do all of it.

Turns out that is the shortest path from here to where you want to go.

The problem is there are so many to choose from that we all get distracted and start to choose like it's some sort of cafeteria. A piece from this person, and a piece from that person, and we'll add a little of this system and a little of that.

Turns out that's called goulash. An awesome Hungarian meal, but a terrible way to run a business.

Want the easiest path we've found in all of our 125 years of work experience? Follow the 6 Step model. ALL of it, not parts.

40
I CHOOSE TO INDULGE IN...

Brad Sugars made this comment at one of the MasterCLASSes he taught this year.

"I feel bad, embarrassed, not good enough, broke, unhappy, etc., etc., etc.," is simply you choosing to indulge in those feelings.

That's fine. As long as you're aware that you are making a conscious decision to allow those feelings.

I'm not talking about loss and grief–although the Stoics would say the situation is the same.

I'm talking about the days you feel like something you did embarrassed you, or you felt like you let yourself down somehow.

Those feelings are a choice–100% of the time. And the alternative is to acknowledge what you did or failed to do, and then act in a way that puts it in the past.

I've done plenty of things that seemed totally embarrassing at the time I did them. In retrospect, none of them has had any impact on my life at all. Zero.

I wonder why I thought it important to indulge in self-questioning, embarrassment, and avoiding because none of those things came true.

I guess the ultimate expression of FEAR—False Expectations Appearing Real.

41
SPRINTING VERSUS ENDURANCE

How long can you do each?

I hear the corporate people we coach talking about the topic du jour of "scrums" and "work sprints" and all manner of other things they are doing to get more done.

The thing is, if you're training for speed you don't run 26 miles of sprints back to back. And if you're training for endurance, you almost never run at a flat-out sprint.

I was a weightlifter. When I was going for a new personal best lift (Hey, I know it's vanity, but my PB on bench press was 465 pounds...), I spent 4 months preparing and working up to a single press.

Max effort = very short term.
Prep and Endurance effort = long term.

They both require thoughtful and planned recovery periods.

So, the concept of the sprint in the work environment is cool. As long as you don't set up a rhythm where you think your team can sprint 100% of the time.

Don't forget the recovery period, where all the gains are consolidated and prepped for the next sprint.

42
EXPERIENCE

What is the value of experience?

What is the value of a guide to show you the way through a problem, process, path or predicament?

What is the value of avoiding mistakes, pitfalls, errors and all the cost that goes along with those things?

Interestingly, none of us knows the value someone else places on our shortcuts.

We were in a training session on pricing today. The room was pretty consistent in the fact that the price is the price and if it's not valued by a prospect, that is totally fine. They just don't get the "thing".

But experience is different. Experience is not a "thing" that can be looked at, measured, seen, etc.

So how do you price for your experience? I mentioned the other day that many of us are guilty of using the "anyone can learn how to do this, so I should price it low" model.

The answer to the value of experience is the answer to this question: How much pain is the person in, how bad do they want to get out of it, and how soon do they want to accomplish that?

The higher the answers are on a 1-10 scale, the higher the value of the experience that can show them the right path.

I think this is an important topic to get your head around. How valuable is it to show people shortcuts that get them their time or money back?

43
EVIDENCE BASED DECISION MAKING

If you continually miss your sales number, the evidence says your sales process isn't very good. It needs to be adjusted.

The challenge comes in when you start to buy all the excuses why the sales numbers are being missed and lose sight of the evidence that the process isn't working. You stay with the failing process because you think the excuses won't repeat.

Then they do. And the evidence continues to show that the process doesn't work. And you accept even more elaborate excuses.

At some point, you need to stop, assess the evidence, and test a different approach.

But only if you want to create different results.

44
YOUR BUSINESS CALLED. IT WANTS HELP...

Funny thing about our businesses.

They show all our personal weaknesses and beliefs as well.

No money in your business bank account? Maybe you just haven't grown your money mindset.

My favorite–tough to get employees? Be a better boss.

This is a simple question. If your business could talk, what would it ask for help with?

If you don't exactly know the answer, give us a call and let us ask you a few questions that will figure out what's going on.

45
LESSONS FROM THE GOLF COURSE

Bad shots happen.

Good recoveries don't necessarily follow.

The difference in final score can completely depend on getting your head right as far as recovery shots.

Sometimes, you might even have to go backward a bit to avoid compounding an error which can lead to actual disaster.

When you F something up, stop, think about the best way to get back on course, do that, even if it requires a step back, and get back on track.

Or take out your three wood, whack a tree, bounce directly down behind the trunk, hit it from the wrong side, whack it again, and take an 8.

Your choice at the end of the day.

I'm just going to offer that a bogey is better than a quadruple bogey.

Business or golf. Recover or compound the problem. Choose wisely.

46
GO SMALL AND GO FAST

Aggressive patience.

The basic stance that you'll have to wait for results, but you can't wait around to get started.

While we were recording the Tough Love for Business Podcast yesterday, one of the topics was catalyzing greatness through incremental steps.

The Grand Gesture seems to be a common desire among entrepreneurs. Go big or go home.

But.

In a world where *The Compound Effect*—Darren Hardy, applies, the Grand Gesture is a fallacy. First, it takes forever to get one done. You can literally spend years attempting to set up and accomplish a Grand Gesture.

That is not aggressive patience.

Second, you get one fell swoop to attempt something. One learning opportunity. One really expensive lesson. A single instance of knowledge gain.

The most likely result of a Grand Gesture in business is failure. You simply try to account for too many variables successfully and on the first try.

Alternatively, hurry the hell up and start taking little steps. All the time you spend creating the Grand Gesture could be spent learning lesson after lesson after lesson. Experimenting toward the result you want. Creating momentum and compounding your results.

Speed is life in business. Start now. Imperfectly is fine. Create your initial hypothesis and test toward it. Now.

The patience part is it will take a little bit to get the result, but it will be worth it.

Or do the Grand Gesture. It's up to you to choose.

47
BREAKTHROUGH

We have a core mindset slide in our system that says a breakthrough must follow a break-up, a break-down, a break-with or a break-apart.

On that basis, we're experiencing breakthroughs in our business processes approximately continuously.

In the past, that sense of unease would have been interpreted as chaos and stopped us in our tracks.

Our child minds would convince us that if we didn't stop until we fixed everything, something horrific would happen.

Uhhh. Nope.

That was our child mind trying to keep us at the same size we were back then. Our comfort zone at that time.

It is exactly as easy to decide that a break-down starts something great as it is to decide you must stop and fix it.

Yes, you'll need to address and upgrade that system to support your new growth. Of course, that will happen. Unless you choose to stay put. Grow or die and all that.

Right now, even as we see more and more things to fix, what is happening is breakthrough after breakthrough.

A system to onboard more people faster? Check.

Better bookkeeping systems? Check.

More clarity on our USP? Check, check, check.

Look, I never said business was easy. Just that it is the best game on the planet, and we are playing it in the best location in the world.

Enjoy the breakthroughs!

48
PERTURBATION

I mentioned that I love perturbation yesterday.

As a reminder, in humans, perturbation often appears as fear, anxiety, anger, frustration, or any of several perceived negative emotions.

What is happening is that you are finding the edge of a comfort zone. You're getting a message, delivered via emotion, that can be summed up as "do you really want to do this?"

Your child mind is throwing up as many blocks to you as it can come up with. Trying to scare you back into staying put. Stasis. Status quo.

That's all. All those negative emotions are working to keep you from growing.

I love it because the other side of perturbation is something new. Opportunities that aren't available to me where I am. Situations that I could not find myself in if I stay in my comfort zone.

Another step up the mountain if you will. Remember, every step up the mountain you take, fewer people will go alongside. The air up top is clean, clear, and refreshing.

All of this is available to you and me if we choose to allow and thrive in perturbation.

49
THERE IS ALWAYS PAIN

When you're broke, you suffer the pain of the grind to get the things you want. When you have the things you want, you suffer the even greater pain of the fear of losing what you've gotten.

Will Smith said that or something similar.

It's likely the best explanation of the "never good enough" syndrome that I have heard.

I have never been a "celebrator". I know the next challenge is coming no matter what I achieve.

That has happened more and more often over the past two years. Our business has set record after record for revenue, growth, clients and more.

In the scope of our "Grand Dream Goal", it's not enough.

But the shift for me is that I am, more and more often, realizing that each step required and accomplished is fulfilling in and of itself. I can still welcome the next challenge while acknowledging the win found within each of those steps.

Enjoy the journey and all that.

And then it finally hit me full force. I love living in perturbation. I love knowing that it means I am experiencing growth in some area, and I love knowing that something cool is around the corner.

It's not easy. I still suffer what I would have called the pain of the grind in the past.

I simply repackaged it as the work of the climb.

50
WHY?

Why choose the harder path?

Why choose to skip over becoming better at owning your business or leading your people?

Why actively participate in ignoring the simple skills yet complaining about your results?

Why hang around Eeyore and his accomplices trying to get you to see the world through their disastrously inaccurate glasses?

Imagine a world where you get up every day, meditate for 10 minutes, read 10 pages of a book, journal a little bit, and then have a cup of coffee.

That is the exact blueprint for a powerful start to your day. Specific, easy to follow, and results based.

Come to think of it, it's not actually the easier path though, is it? It would still be easier to lay in bed a few more minutes, starting yourself off on a path to complain and wonder all day why things aren't how you "want" them.

Choose wisely.

51
THE QUALITY OF YOUR OUTPUT

Your business, your customer experience, your financial results.

The quality of any of these items cannot exceed the quality of the lowest performer on your team.

Still think it's ok to keep that one slacker around?

Still believe that it's not worth becoming good at hiring? Because it's "too hard?"

Still believe that your team will compensate for that person who half asses things all day?

You just keep on keeping on then.

52
CLEAN YOUR MIND

Darren Hardy uses an example of the kind of junk we can accept into our brains by filling a glass with cola.

Hard to see through the glass when it's full of dark, opaque liquid. The news. "Reality." What the most recent politician said. What someone said or showed on "the facebook."

All of that is like pouring that dark, impossible to see through cola into your brain and then trying to see through it to possibilities and optimism.

Doesn't work. All of that shit is designed to hijack your amygdala, which is always scanning for danger. The way to get your eyes, if you let them, is to make every possible thing appear as scary as it possibly can.

He further shares how to clean your mind by pouring in fresh, clear water and flushing the garbage.

Here's the rub. It takes 5-15 times as much water as sludge to get the water in the glass to replace the cola completely.

And just like showering, flushing the crap out of your mind isn't a one and done activity.

Every day. Every time you look at social media or watch the news or listen to a political "commentator" of some sort, you're dumping sludge back into your brain.

And every day you'll need to keep flushing it with massive amounts of clean, clear water.

Protect your mind. You only have one!

ADDITIONAL RESOURCES

Subscribe to Mike's daily email blog. A 37 second or less daily read with Mike's thoughts on business, leadership, and just being a good human at **ActionCOACHWI.com/daily-dose-of-business/**

Listen to our podcast where we provide a little Tough Love for Business Owners and address the rules of the game of business at **actioncoachwi.com/tough-love-for-business-podcast/**

Your Business CAN Be a Commercial Profitable Enterprise That Works Without You

A simple promise.
You can have a great business and a great life.

Talk with one of our coaches about one issue in your business and a complementary Coaching Session
actioncoachwi.com/book_strategy_session

In business, it is always the little things that get the big results. Our Business Health Check will give you invaluable insights into the many areas of your business. By completing the Business Health Check, you will receive a Free Report based on your answers, prepared by our team of highly skilled Business Coaches.

Get your Business Health Check at
actioncoachwi.6stepsscorecard.com

ABOUT THE AUTHOR

Mike McKay is a globally renowned Business and Executive Coach as a multi-year winner of Global Executive Coach of the Year from ActionCOACH. He is a US Army veteran and an ActionCOACH Global Hall of Fame Member, but most importantly, Mike is a husband and father of four.

Mike has worked with businesses ranging from 2-20,000 employees and uses a unique framework for business growth and acceleration only available through ActionCOACH Licensed coaches.

Mike has coached in three countries and spoken on 3 continents. He's co-host of the Tough Love for Business Podcast, the author of th eDaily Dose of Business Blog, and the owner of ActionCOACH Milwaukee.

Mike is a proud graduate of Ripon College in Wisconsin, with a degree in Math, and a huge Green Bay Packer fan.

www.ingramcontent.com/pod-product-compliance
Lightning Source LLC
Chambersburg PA
CBHW072017230526
45479CB00008B/191